Michelle Koch

JUST
ONE
MORE

Greenwillow Books
New York

Watercolor paints were used for the full-color art.
The text type is ITC Symbol.

Printed in Singapore by Tien Wah Press

First Edition 10 9 8 7 6 5 4 3 2 1

Library of Congress Cataloging-in-Publication Data
Koch, Michelle.
Just one more / by Michelle Koch.
p.   cm.
Summary: Labelled pairs of illustrations explore
the plural forms of irregular nouns such as
child/children, goose/geese, and leaf/leaves.
ISBN 0-688-08127-4.
ISBN 0-688-08128-2 (lib. bdg.)
1. English language – Noun – Juvenile literature.
2. English language – Number – Juvenile literature.
[1. English language – Noun.
2. English language – Number.] I. Title.
PE1216.K63 1989 428.1 – dc19
88-17736 CIP AC

For Sna and Bobby

child

children

goose

geese

moose

moose

leaf

leaves

oxen

knife

knives

foot

feet

mouse

mice

deer

deer

man

men

loaf

loaves

wolf

wolves

one . . . and more

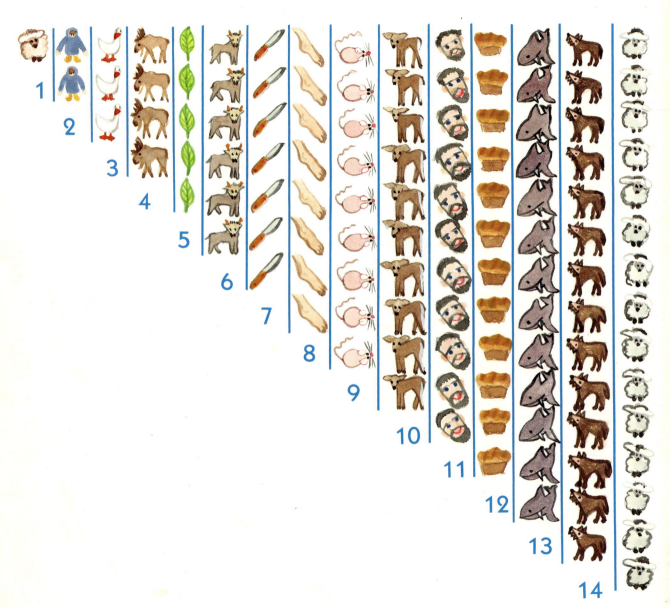

1
2
3
4
5
6
7
8
9
10
11
12
13
14
15